OPTION THREE

James Hamilton-Paterson

LONDON
VICTOR GOLLANCZ LTD
1974

© James Hamilton-Paterson 1974
ISBN 0 575 01891 7

Printed in Great Britain by
The Camelot Press Ltd, Southampton

For

ANN and JONATHAN WORDSWORTH

ACKNOWLEDGEMENT

The poem 'Anthony Prince' first appeared in *The Poetry Review*

Contents

OPTION THREE

Anthony Prince

You are dying, and ten years old.
We both know this. It remains therefore
for me to speed you on your way
with words; an overwrought but cold
elegy, perhaps, mapping the route to your
small grave like the nurse each day
with your charted blood; a few glib lines
about your youth and innocence,
reflecting that God's laws at times
seem cruelly devoid of sense.

And all that stuff about our souls
in radiance at the mercy-seat,
whatever that may be; I think
we shall never in our separate holes
see each other. What is complete
is that we met before the brink.
Let no one say because a boy
shall die a huge voice must speak
from the air, or that it means a toy
has fallen, outgrown, at those far feet.

Kindergarten Art Exhibition

Eventually, I get too morose and bored
to go on shuffling sideways through the classrooms,
staring at migraines of strident poster-colour
crowded on to coarse grey sketching paper;
stick-men crucified to a violet sky,
women dressed in pyramids, and cows
like vaulting-horses pinning down the grass.

I wonder, in fact, if children see the world
in leaping perspective, or if they simply move
between walls of colour stencilled into shapes
where everyone has a polio victim hunch,
like knights on mediaeval tapestries
riding flat horses on an upright field.

For sometimes even now the streets can frame
such nursery crowds. Horizons stand on end
like street artists' slabs, and indentical cut-out men
hold hands eternally as they pull apart.
On such a day the colours shout and run
but never touch me, standing dull and chilled
beneath the orange sun glued to the sky.

Me, Toad

You, who move me under the skin
where my beauty ends, do not mock
my jumping heart, my ugly grin,
my hunched and watchful mind, nor lock
your petshop collar round my brain;
but as you wander through your field
of chosen plunder where you kissed
before you mauled, look round again:
it is not only toads who die
miserably in the harrow's fist.

poem

ribs on a beach
boat or man
tell us all that sailors can.

bones in a field
ox or youth
lie round ploughmen as the truth.

what is soft
and can be bruised
holds the whip or is abused.

how they captained
how they ruled
how they pondered how they muled

may be written/
lost by chance:
years digest irrelevance.

latin lesson

of course it's not
dead they said
because you start right in
with thrills: practically learn
to run before you walk.
ignore but memorise

the first word
amo i love.
altogether now
i thou he-she-or-it
we you (pl.) they.
amant: everybody's doing it

but not for long.
from dusty scabbards
flash real weapons
across the pages
flee slaves and enemies
dying in every tense.

even at the end
citadels still fall
and generals
command the last attack
but more long-windedly
and sometimes conditionally.

they wield death
in sentences
by with or from a horse
often in a camp.
balbus slept here
is not scratched

on a wall and
caesar is not mentioned
in despatches as
small bald and queer.
only the stark downpour
of darts and the terror of horses

and the barbarians who were
or were not
about to be or thought
to be about to be
killing MDCCC prisoners or
hostages ad lib.

simpler to ride
with caesar and his soldier's
plain language:
to follow brilliant campaigns
than parse tricky things
by catullus

poems about kisses.
hard to believe that any
red blooded boy would rather
wander with lesbia through
lemon groves than
run with cohorts

Song 1

Walking across this beloved field
so often, hazel heart
twisting in my hands,
divining beneath a certain part
the mineral vein of love
buried deeper than hurt.
Love, I am unsure to dig,
knowing pride alone
bends any dowser's twig.

Stupid to think what's true for me
is true for any other;
that beyond the window
an indefatigable lover
walks up and down.
Now I ought rather
to listen to the inner, discreet
rain of tissues dying
than the soundless street.

Little mad girl

I doubt very much if your rolled eyes
see bright, kind faces over the bed,
or dark dreams when the tired nurse
hears whimpering in the rigid night.
You cry, not under saddened lids
but because some synapse deep inside
dictates so of its own mad will;
then wildly grin and wave your tongue
and move your bowels in sympathy.

Yet yours is not the tragedy;
the flaw that judders you in this cot
neither disgusts nor frightens me.
But in your father's eyes vibrates
a fear of which I am afraid;
for when I watch your fingers crawl
across the sheet towards his sleeve
I see him cringe and not dare touch
the groping insect of your hand.

Hinksey Pool

The tension
of sunlight
pulls me away from how
I never was; my eyes
stare down, my clothes are kind to me.

Can't pass
a swimming-pool
on summer walks, but skirt
a leaden confrontation
hastily through dusty streets.

Love, if those
unknown bathers
multiplied your beauty
into commonness!
But their pink festivities

celebrate
the body that
I held. So little pain
is meanly saved by knowing
of our plunging transience,

how perhaps
they'll need to be
helped into buses by
the now unborn; for we
shall both have finished travelling.

Wintrily distant,
passing through,
moved hopelessly to watch
the bright skins which separate
our individual darknesses.

Herd

Being brought up to carry arms
from our loaded childhoods
harms our touching and our seeing.

Feel how fingers curl, observe
our eyes narrow; notice
nerves that keep us wary peel.

Still in this bovine regiment
which drills to inner shouts,
intent and practising to kill,

I sit slowly down at last
disarmed by sudden spleen,
past bearing my own cruelty.

Which would they rather I pulled, a gun
or a coin? The violence I have
done with banknotes, stamping rich

shoes through poor lands: it will
outlive me and, recalled,
fill arsenals with such values.

life sentence

a long
solitary
stretch

sometimes cornered
in the library
for a recital
on a stone organ
as tall ranks of
lapidary books
exhort and drone

in the time
it takes the eyes
to feel their way
down each
incised page
2,000 as yet
unessential components
of the brain
die

the grammes of dead matter
in the skull
add yearly
the creeping blankness
accretes
in grey pebbles

thinking grates
deeply against them
like a pudding knife
on plum stones

before long
the weight
will ballast the head and
our necks lug fossils

sometimes working all day
at the rock mines
among the knock and split
of heads
for something that will
outlast stone

but
every night
hearing the other
prisoners of chemistry
tapping on
each other's walls
the message of
our brief
conjunction
of cells

Song 2

Years won't reassure which
ending youth bring emptiness.
Sands run out, hopes lag behind.

Before the earth plugs up our ears:
the slow moult and the leaking;
the stiffening, the foxed hands.

From Penang Hill

Sometimes when the wind
turns a corner
the sounds of town come up.
Otherwise, a dead world
drowned in distance,
a view.
From underfoot slides
the slow glacier of trees
and round the bottom
a moraine city lies
where there are no people
and where the slums
are clean out of sight;
only the white cubes
and cylinders of commerce
bare their far teeth.

Why when we walked together
was it mostly upwards?
For meanness swallowed
by perspective, for all
that could be overlooked?
If to preserve ourselves,
then far now from those
high wanderings I stand
and have not changed.
With unsought constancy
alone and somewhere
up on the earth's crust,
watching down a precipice of air
geometry fed by threads
of fossil rivers. But all

I see is the inside of your
elbow, leaning on a parapet ago,
your almost child's skin
translucent, and underneath
a blue vein.

at this point

at this point
the garden meets the empty sea
the pressure to speak is less
and how I spend my time
only the sea knows

surprising
now you have left
how little there is to say

I read long books
alone
in spring and
in autumn write dull letters
and watch the birds leave

I am powerless now
as I shall be
to speak truly about pain

something which is an absence
and which does not end
eats its own tail
dumbly

neither do we have
the power to write
about our pain:
the enormous impotence leaks out
in slow words on to the page
like women crying in their sleep

our happiness together
was the sum of our small moments
of not remembering:
the birds distilled their sound
in drops
and we forgot
not even our held hands
will stop us falling

I shall go back
to being an Englishman
and in due course will die
an English death

I will sit in warm post offices
and shuffle round libraries
in a dejected mackintosh
looking for novels with large print
whose pages smell of biscuit crumbs

my nib will wander in spikes:
shallow electric waves
dying on an endless shore of paper
as my brain nods
heavy and old on its stem
like a blown peony

moons will whirl
and clouds stalk on rain
the sky be smudged with birds
and the sea wash its hands of us
while I
with spectacles and blue veins
will not be able to remember
what I once read in spring
nor those I wrote to
in autumn

In your garden

Flowers advertise
themselves. I don't need a
guide to help me see
tulips, honesty or
rue; the way that buddleia
glowers tells me more than
you. I nod but really
watch your neat jungle
hide every grain of
soil (as your wealth in
showers

brims your house: not an
inch uncarpeted, no
shelf unornamented).

Stand at the garden gate,
jail your ego and look
in at yourself. See the
grey virgin pose
among his evergreens and
fail to blend; hear his
tongue cut and dig
away dead cronies,
reveal spermatic exploits,
rail at those who weren't
so desperately deceived.

Listen: in the digging is the clink
of struck flints. It is fair we should
be known by the gardens that we keep.
Beneath the riot of verbiage
the starkness lies like earth;

words and flowers blossom to conceal
their common origin: relentlessly
the blooms articulate,
their magnificent shouts betray
all the uneasy places.

Remember, when your treasured
spinney has been chopped
down, the lawn ploughed
up to build a new
school, the very last
ember of your fig-tree's
cool and your mopes
about the death of elegance
shown to be at least
the weeding-out of privilege,
remember:

they will want to know
what seed took root,
whom you made happy.

Presently, when you are
humus and the rabble
has inherited your
private earth, children's
hands may rake your very
animus for tests, your
lands dissolving as they
titrate and shake you gently
in a flask, dip blue
litmus, watch your final
acids deeply blush.

Song 3

My turning sun
it's no great light you shed;
eclipses and the null rains come
as ever on this head, but now
whole days disclose themselves
in despite.

And wandering
soon over the horizon
to another's hollows, leaves
such wry wondering at how
there is no risen light
but dark follows.

Volcano in El Salvador

From the lip of the crater
the trees pour down, a perfect
green cone. Only a few years ago
lava like grey pus ran;
shrubs exploded, firecrackers
descending the hill until it stood
bare and silent.
              Now the leaves
are back: a sudden shower
of seeds from the tropic air,
a sometime volcano becomes
a temporary hill. People
walk on it and forget. They
grow maize on it; their
children burst from the soil.
I watch the thick trees hold
thousands of tons of sap
in the air.
            Half a hemisphere
away, a land last menaced by
glaciers and stagnant with unchange.
Being made young by foreignness
is suddenly to disdain those
cool pastures, the single trees
dying of lightning and worms.

Logging at Grassguards
(for Jonathan)

With jokes and blades we
draw the wet woods, searching
for later warmth. The banter hides
fondly our pride in being alone
and separate, the cool asides
ward off devastation, touching,
then unexpectedly

finding nearness
peels away a tender blaze
to mark the cut. Only the calm
exult of lying in the sun
with friends can so much overwhelm:
sleep on the shared grass a daze
of belonging less,

because the bright
devil crawls inside and sours,
nags of the inward slow walk
to isolation and the one
life beyond the reach of talk,
lived alone in sullen hours
of squandered light.

Now the rust-
raw rip of teeth shall bind,
the cutting join us. Living lumps
spray our wrists and fall as bone.
Through the waiting forest stumps
war with axes; on the wind
drifts our dust.

At Dawn

At dawn
the quiet spill of the sun
down the screes catches sheep
in their night postures.
Under the fells nothing moves
but the brief, indelible
flare of your hands
slicing beets, instantly
eclipsed by common light.

All long ago. It
makes no sense, time,
which so weathers with
casual desolation and in
the night hours shrinks men
to incredulous dots.
Since the held flash
of your wet knife
froze me in parentheses
I have wandered headless
through wastes of others'
moments. There should be
more to life than elegy;
but wherever you are,
whatever loss of time,
nothing has come of the
wait for dazzling
coincidence. You never have
recurred. No secret how
the sun rose only
on a single morning
to so stop sheep in their
tracks, so to dispose

shadow and cloud among
wide bulks of stone.

The time is gone, you
would mistake the place.
Those sheep are dead;
that bracken humus; new
rocks have since congealed
from interstellar dust.
Among the fells my nights
are loose with distance
and the quiet goes out
in all directions. Closed
from walking in the dark
down from the hills
and mute with time I
open my cold mouth
silently on the
valueless breaking day.
The trees emerge, are jets
of wood forced by old
pressures through the ground.
At the huge halt of dawn
we wait in the fossil air.

An Evening's Fiction

Oh, fires and wine and jokes
and banished horrors hanging
round the door like maniac bears;

congenial silence is alone
enough to drown the cold
rush of starlight over the slates.

When singly and for ever
each friend steps
unseeing out past bears and stars,

there should be a sharp sound
as of air imploding,
a new unwelcome atmosphere

will stand or sit or not drink wine
among us. Now how long
before this blank intruder spoils

affectionate games of shutting out
the primal beast who makes
occupied spaces go to wind?

Wits with dying follicles.
An untruth for the sake
of play could be too late for words.

When our last vacuum fills
unheard, the warmth will drain
from the house, the desolate rooms hiss

with rays snagging the chipped wedge
of roof as it parts
lines of light from the Milky Way.

may morning 1969

it does no good
each year asking for it all
to wait
wanting to catch up
take part

remorselessly
and in such light and unison
grass begets grass
oaks spawn acorns
in effortless prodigality

each egg and bud
bursts with what scientists call
the best-kept secret

people are always talking
about the secret of life

there are no secrets
only what is too common
for notice
too plain to be understood
there are no secrets for us
only the endless possibilities
for treason

while our thin bones hold us
inches above the soil
the facts which matter are

perennially there
about our final refusal
to hold each other
about there one day being
no more sun

I hate to be touched

I hate to be touched
except by those who know
the stones will win;
whose lives are not worth
a bag of shit sprouting from
the lower abdomen;
who find a single killed father
unwrites symphonies, unravels sonnets
into lying odds and ends.

I hate to be touched
except by those who know
where the war is;
who are wary of love,
bored by God and cash, but leap
for sheer precariousness;
those who know the flare of private
revelation will not light the world's
dark necessary march:

those touch me.

Poem for Ann

For many years nobody lived
in the other house on the hill.
Alone, I moved with the slow shift
of constant things: eddies of grey
sheep around the stones
and tides of wind.

When there was most sun
my winter thoughts
hung in the air. I was
a bomb of darkness and this sun
burned away my time on
a shortening fuse.

Now, when night silts up
the valley, climbs the slope,
creeps over sills and drowns
our roofs, your lights
sail out like square moons,
primordial and familiar.

We don't look closely at each other
but keep our humming distance
like telegraph poles. Habits
of silence soon identify the tone
at which we resonate,
the sound autumn falls to.

I am in the hills because
everybody talks. No need to send
messages across: hum in the wind
and keep the silence. We
shall hear high songs
in our visionary ears.

Our tuned houses ring;
behind the stuffy wainscots
light mice run.
Let summer open windows
in our heads: see how
our love puffs out like curtains.

Thomas Spence

Behind the drained fens
a black rim of dyke. Among
the stiff fields huddle
cottages without roofs,
emptied by tides and absent
ownership. Here
unrecorded labourers leaned
against the sea. Stupefied
by mystery they vanished as
their own work evicted them;
another's crops and the inland
flowers are their testimony.

Elsewhere the tumult
and the cities rise up. There
is nothing more to learn
from woods and fields;
they have deserted us,
twinkling and brooding,
exhaling dawns like cattle.
Now land and landlord wield
tyrannical indifference. Learn
from one the deep stupidity
of miracle; in the other see
prospects for rebellion.

Or each single life
drudges to the grave. Plugging
the hole through which the heart
jets, the salt tonnage
held back—this unpaid
labour will reclaim its
angry freehold. All rural

43

harmony enslaves: nothing now
so clear as while the
wrested land dumbly speaks
its seeds, one only master
grasps the whole domain.

Spence (1750–1814) was a radical bookseller and inventor of a scheme for land nationalisation. In 1792 he moved to London where he was later imprisoned for selling Paine's Rights of Man.

conversation with a mirror

you are not there
I cannot see you
taste you
hear you
feel you
nobody can touch you

unperson
you have planted nothing
in a single field
but luckily the starving
don't know this
so they go on waiting
for the next harvest
and the next
and the next

the political prisoner
after his daily beating
hears the life dripping out of him
running to waste
on the floor of his cell

the pool evaporates
as does yours
but he is given
no choice

your voice is not raised
in protest
and the political prisoner
hears nothing
all day he hears nothing
but new shades of grey
fall like torn-off wings
about his ears

the bonfires of children
are well alight around the world
bright hayricks in a dark landscape
you have sprinkled not one drop
to put out the smallest toe
or smouldering ear
not one foot have you pulled
from the charring

your fastidiousness
makes the children who meet you
likely candidates to fill
future vacancies
in the ranks
of pitchfork-wielders

in a year or two
you will not be there in the morning
when you carefully back
your car
out of the garage

safe
inside it
with the windows shut
the doors locked
you will be a driver
you will be nobody

you won't be there in the day
you'll be a voice on a telephone
you won't be there at night
you'll be an eater of dinners
a watcher of television

you can't be found now
and soon
the hungry people
the political prisoners
the children who tomorrow will be embers
will give up looking for you
listening
waiting

they will be excused for thinking
you don't exist
except that if you didn't
they wouldn't be starving
jailed
burning

when eventually
and it may be next week
your medical insurance company
has to pay up
you'll lie exsanguinated
in your dried-up pool
and your attentive nurses themselves
will be hard put to decide
when you are too absent even
to close your own eyes

a last word to the mandarin who wears my clothes

because people don't wear shoes
and particularly boots
in your presence
no mud is brought in and
you are surrounded by silence
sitting all day
robed in mystification

all day contained
by books and ivory
your white hands clicking
with nail
your gestures larded
with prerogative

the true ignorance of the exalted
is yours
the minute knowledge of your library
is yours
the intimacy of your jade
is yours
as is your serene accompaniment
of yourself
on your delicate instrument

now you may be moved
to add to the literature
of your kingdom

with precise strokes
brush on the precious ink
unknowing that at every drop
an unwashed head
falls to blackness

for all those who live
as mandarins
a million think
but nobody downs tools to watch
rich lonely children
elegantly playing tag
on a private playground
of allusion

every one
with a faraway look and soft clothes
celebrates in his cadences
the unafforded luxury
of being bourgeois

never love or death
only points scored
and grazed knees

you have no violence to fear

a few students may knock
your hat off and daub
slogans on your palace walls
interrupt your masturbation

no mob will come

you will simply be
left out in the rain
to die in thin elegiacs
of literary suffering

Option Three
(12 poems written in Indochina, 1971)

I

Understand
that there were only extremes left.
That in terms of pure sound
there was nothing now between
painstaking symphonics and
the squeak of scuffed sand.

Understand
that there were no more places left;
that each remoter landscape grown
to resonate to unfamiliar tongues
gave out silence and
his own image back.

Understand
that faced with casual desolation
there was nothing to expect;
nothing to pass but palest days
amounting to the white
monument of age.

Understand
that Option Three* was complicity,
and the body might as well
have stopped. But
there was a growth, a furious
nodule having more life
than its host. Its pillow
was soaked but
it could not be kept private.

* 'Option Three' is White House jargon for compromise.

Sometimes it spilled its blood
in public, on restaurant tables,
in subways, in corners
of parks.

2

Understand
there is no road left between
the brutish and the sentimental;
yet spent poets
invent new monsters.

We are through with myth
and metaphor. In particular
there are no phoenixes.
As for the tired sea, it
has been dredged and dredged again;
has been sailed with
charged galleys, has changed
sex a thousand times, has
been harvested with every tide
for its beached skeletons.

Poetry is nearly at an end.
It was a language of aspiration,
of ignorance made elegant.
Too many facts are known,
too many truths too bald
and too unrhymable.

It must be known:
there is no God,
there are no flags, there can be
no brotherhood of man;
we
can love one another and die.
The rich explain the poor,
and only the very wealthiest meek
could inherit the earth.

The miracle dandies have sat
alone in their towers.
They have found the last
and most true celebration
of humanity in books.
They have cried for the past
and themselves. They
weep more for Little Nell
than for the children burned
by ambassadors.

What wasted tears oh
what wasted tears.
How weeping for all
conceals self-pity.
The drops added each to each
would nearly make a metaphor.
What wasted tears.
What wasted tears.

3

We are nearly at an end.
Tombs outlive their pity; and now
with urgent and unwasted rage
the need to undeceive.

Moneyed wars are fought;
in the capitals they
have not yet been told
the body-counts are fixed.

Tombs outlive their pity. The
young men burst by bullets
and all those without graves,
they cover the earth: their
poppies sweat remembrance.

Honour honour honour

Honour is to be the old,
the cancerous, the ordinarily dead.
Tombs outlive their pity; greater
lies are written there than ever
send each stone its foot of clay.

They cover the earth: their poppies
ooze the people's drug
which cancels anger, paralyses
brains. So have lived

To hear the killed in combat figures
declared acceptable. Oh blank
and bleeding through the mouth, we
are nearly at an end.

4

Seen from an ejector seat
they were unmemorable;
no sooner glimpsed
than left behind,
the prickling instants
hidden by flame when
those who were washing,
picking rice or walking
to school became
fading green blotches
on the retina. Ahead,
the years would drift on,
full of beer and anger
and semen while
the life assurance matured
in a vault and
under the fat the fragile
bones prepared their outliving
silently.

Those who were gentle
and who gave their children
kind egress into an indifferent world
are forgotten,

the statues of yesterday's
honoured louts
are cleared for runways,

the heads of the brilliant
and the touched
are full of roots

and those who gave
blackness its voice are themselves
benighted in anthologies.

All is as it should be,
for little counts but present cruelty.

This is my language;
I speak it haltingly.
I have watched while
they outlawed disaffection;
I saw the miraculous
unvanishing of the poor;
I heard the statistics
of child mortality proclaimed
satisfactory; witnessed
the enviable envy of the rich
for the richer, the reverent
silence of bystanders
leaning on their hired spades.

Soon one day spring
will be long overdue and
the birds will have turned to stone.
Peasants squat in the shadow
of imperial junketings,
whittling sticks and waiting
for the relief trucks.
Charity and unchangingness
deserve the utmost savagery;
there is no other language which
can comprehend white phosphorus.
All history is as if
not one tear had ever been shed.

Beneath the brilliant lights
his body lay emptied, stacks of
bone in one sterile drum; bowel
floating in a pan; muscle, lungs
and lights in separate jars. In
the rummaged hide were pins to
lay flat what tried to curl, and
massively expose to scrutiny
his hollowness. Consultation
followed minute probings, for
from oesophagus to ankles not
a cell was out of place, far less
a nodule as obvious as a growth.

Loath to fail, they all tried to
guess where it hid and where it
got its blood. Something their
raw clearances, their closest
examinations had overlooked—
tiny and forgotten, a marooned
island of self—lay in its skull,
two tears sparkling under the
thin slits. *The head,* they cried;
*tongues and brains often have
foul tumours. The head.* So trays
of new blades came. The initial
bites were made with rongeurs.

8

Slept deeply was dark and its panics:
it gathered from the extinguished
light of immense multitudes. Most had
perished soundlessly; a few had lit
wicks in the void or eloquently wept.

Sad terrors of violence and ageing
find living echoes. Some, on catching
sight of meat or mirror, cannot ignore
seeing bombs fall like hair and send
raging pity into the sky. Many go mad.

Your children will vanish, as him you
hold in your arms. He who hopes there
might be company is lost. There is only
bare commonness in being human: old,
new, or bleakly registering the hour.

Which was how they found **him,**
beached on one elbow,
hair flat and mouth
plugged with shingle, nothing
but horizons all
around and the sea
smooth as cropped turf.
He opened colourless eyes
which were to have been
pressed by infinite salt,
saw only the silent
ring of those who stood.
From his hanging mouth
stones fell and shells
and threads of seaweed. It
was all he had to say.
His antrums, sinuses
and ears full, his head
rang like a flask.
Faintly their whispers blew
past him. One of them said:
There are no accidents,
and he acknowledged it was
true as anything he had
found caught in the hinges
of the sea.
          When
they left, their feet had made
no pattern of the scuffed
sand but he could see,
through mucus, not
a grain was out of place.
Time passed and the gulls

left him as the light
dimmed and even the crabs
mustered unseen their brittle
army to peel his face.
But they came out with the stars,
and carefully the moon
drew water over his head.

there was a cat opposite
in the sun walking by a wall,
made love to an iron bolt.

time melted. rubbing its
head its neck its ears over
the luxurious six edges.

bemused by finding such
silent affection it moved
away with its tail stiff.

but
no bought silence
can muffle how earth turns
to ancient unaccidental sounds.
each new day hemp creaks,
dawn breaks
to a snap of necks and
bowels drench.

something
they did, something
they said, something they were.
miraculous it did not happen sooner.
elsewhere their unknown friends who
won't be bought,
will not accommodate or lie,
listen with furious love as the sun comes up,

for
they have last words,
those silent prisoners who fill our waking
with their wet involuntary sounds.
proudly they tell of how, mulish
with spleen and questions
they shall forever hang insoluble
in the lightless brilliance
of the void.

Most mornings now
I function as an ear, and lest
we grow aloof in the long noons
of disaffection, we can find
lost nights occasionally:

proof that days we
thought this mutual ground
we trod or lay on, love, bore us up
are bliss outdated—a gentle
roof of sheltered history.

For my skull fills
with immense cries. Distant
digging of vast pits shakes me;
I sense little but the brute
raw nearing of excavation.

Past touchings of
hands count for nothing now;
only sounds of present endings
will amount. Love, I shall not
last. Slowly I am darkening.